M000311879

SCARY SPICE
IN MY POCKET

MEL B

SMITHMARK

Photographs: All Action – back cover, 3, 6, 9, 13, 14, 17, 18, 21, 22 & 23, 24 & 25, 28 Capital Pictures – 4, 11, 17, 27, 31, 33, 34, 36, 40, 43, 44, 47, 48 Retna – front cover, endpapers, 1, 39

This edition published in 1997 by SMITHMARK Publishers, a division of U.S. Media Holdings, Inc., 115 West 18th Street, New York, NY 10011.

SMITHMARK books are available for bulk purchase for sales promotion and premium use. For details write or call the manager of special sales, SMITHMARK Publishers, 115 West 18th Street, New York, NY 10011.

Design by Blackjacks

Concept by Clare Hulton

ISBN 0-7651-9129-6

Printed in Singapore

1 0 9 8 7 6 5 4 3 2 1

Library of Congress CIP

Neither the members of the Spice Girls nor any of their representatives have had any involvement with this book.

Full name:
Melanie Janine Brown

Date of birth: 29 May 1975

Distinguishing marks:
A pierced tongue and a
Japanese tattoo

Height: 5ft 5in

'I'D LIKE TO THINK
MY TALENT IS
GIVING EVERY
PERSON I COME
INTO CONTACT WITH
THAT LITTLE BIT OF
ZEST FOR LIFE
AGAIN.'

MEL B PAID HER WAY THROUGH DANCE SCHOOL BY PERFORMING AT A CLUB IN LEEDS FOR £2.50 PER HOUR

MEL B IS A SELF-CONFESSED NUTTER

ACCORDING TO EMMA, MEL B IS REALLY TERRIBLE IN THE MORNINGS AND A TOTAL HYPOCHONDRIAC AS WELL

SCARY SPICE THINKS JAY K FROM JAMIROQUAI IS 'DAMN SEXY'. 'GIVE HIM TO ME' SHE PROCLAIMED IN A RECENT TV DOCUMENTARY

MEL B'S PAST CAREER INCLUDES A BRIEF APPEARANCE IN 'CORONATION STREET' AND PLAYING THE DRUMS AT MUSIC SCHOOL. WHEN SHE WAS EIGHTEEN SHE WON A BEAUTY CONTEST – THE PRIZE WAS A CAR

SCARY SPICE'S IDEAL MAN MUST BE ZANY AND SPONTANEOUS

WHEN MEL B'S FLAT WAS DESTROYED BY FIRE LAST YEAR, SHE MANAGED TO ESCAPE IN HER NIGHT-CLOTHES BUT LOST MANY OF HER POSSESSIONS, INCLUDING SOME SPICE GIRLS GOLD DISCS

**SCARY
SPICE
RECKONS
'YOU CAN
GET AWAY
WITH
ANYTHING
AS LONG
AS YOU'RE
CHEEKY'**

MEL B
HATES WEAK
MEN AND
SALADS

SCARY SPICE'S NICKNAME USED TO BE PINEAPPLE HEAD

'I DON'T DO QUIET'

MEL B WAS 'SPECTACLE WEARER OF THE YEAR' IN 1997

'BOYFRIENDS SHOULD NEVER RULE YOUR LIFE OR COME BETWEEN YOU AND YOUR FRIENDS'

SCARY SPICE'S FAVOURITE WORDS ARE HIGGLEDY-PIGGLEDY AND HOTCH-POTCH

MEL B'S MUM CRIED WHEN SHE WATCHED HER 'LITTLE GIRL' ON STAGE AT THE SPICE GIRLS' FIRST BRIT AWARDS

ON CHATTING UP
MEN MEL B SAYS,
'DO IT WITH CHICK
STYLE AND BOLDNESS.
"I FANCY YOU, I DO"
— IT'S A KILLER!'

MEL B
ONCE HAD
A JOB IN
PANTOMIME
IN LONDON
– BUT SHE
GOT SACKED
FOR
GIGGLING
ALL THE
TIME!

MEL B IS THE SPICE GIRL WITH BIG HAIR. 'EVERY BAND NEEDS BIG HAIR,' SAYS MEL

MEL B LOVES TO GO CLUBBING ... AND HER FAVE TELEVISION PROGRAMME IS 'ANYTHING ABOUT CLUBBING'